Metaverse

What it is? How to Invest in Metaverse and its Future Horizons

by

Phillip Daniels

© Copyright 2022 - All Rights Reserved.

The content contained within this book may not be reproduced, duplicated, or transmitted without direct written permission from the author or the publisher.

Under no circumstances will any blame or legal responsibility be held against the publisher, or author, for any damages, reparation, or monetary loss due to the information contained within this book, either directly or indirectly.

Legal Notice:

This book is copyright protected. It is only for personal use. You cannot amend, distribute, sell, use, quote, or paraphrase any part, or the content within this book, without the consent of the author or publisher.

Disclaimer Notice:

Please note the information contained within this document is for educational and entertainment purposes only. All effort has been executed to present accurate, up-to-date, reliable, and complete information. No warranties of any kind are declared or implied.

Readers acknowledge that the author is not engaged in the rendering of legal, financial, medical, or professional advice. The content within this book has been derived from various sources. Please consult a licensed professional before attempting any techniques outlined in this book.

By reading this document, the reader agrees that under no circumstances is the author responsible for any losses, direct or indirect, that are incurred as a result of the use of the information contained within this document, including, but not limited to, errors, omissions, or inaccuracies.

Table of Contents

Chapter 1: Introduction
- What is the Metaverse?
- What Is the Metaverse All About?
- How does it Work?

Chapter 2: Blockchain and Crypto
- What Role Does Blockchain and Crypto Play In The Metaverse?

Chapter 3: Top 5 Crypto Metaverse Projects
- Sandbox
- Decentraland Marketplace
- Illuvium

Illuvial

Tokenomics

Star Atlas
- $UFO
- Future Predictions

Chapter 4: Top Metaverse Investment Companies
- Qualcomm
- Meta Platforms Inc.
- Amazon
- Microsoft (MSFT)
- Content Creation
- Unity Software (U)
- Autodesk Inc. (ADSK)
- Roblox (RBLX)

- Disney
- Semiconductors
- NVIDIA
- Advanced Micro Devices

Chapter 5: Where To Invest
- Stocks
- Land and Property
- Tokens
- ApeCoin (APE)
- MANA
- Avie Infinity
- NFTs and Wearables
- Potential Markets In The Universe
- Virtual Goods
- Digital Art
- Virtual Real Estate
- Online Gaming
- Construction
- Virtual Events

Chapter 6: Investing Truth: Venture Capital
- How The Metaverse Will Replace Traditional Tech
- How to Invest
- ETFs
- Global X FinTech
- Roundhill Ball Metaverse ETF
- Evolve Metaverse

- Stocks
- Fastly
- Shopify
- Google
- Invest Successfully

Chapter 7: Web 3.0

- Domain Names
- How to Register
- What Is ENS and How Does it Work?

Chapter 8: Metaverse Medical Technology

- Telepresence
- Health Technology
- Digital Twins
- Blockchain Technology
- Convergence

Chapter 9: 2040 Technological Predictions

- Brain-Computer Interface (BCI)
- Service Robots Could Be Used Worldwide
- Quantum Computers
- Lifelike Virtual Assistants Could Be Mainstream
- Einstein Telescope
- Establish the First Permanent Lunar Base
- Deep-sea Mining Operations

Conclusion

References

Chapter 1: Introduction

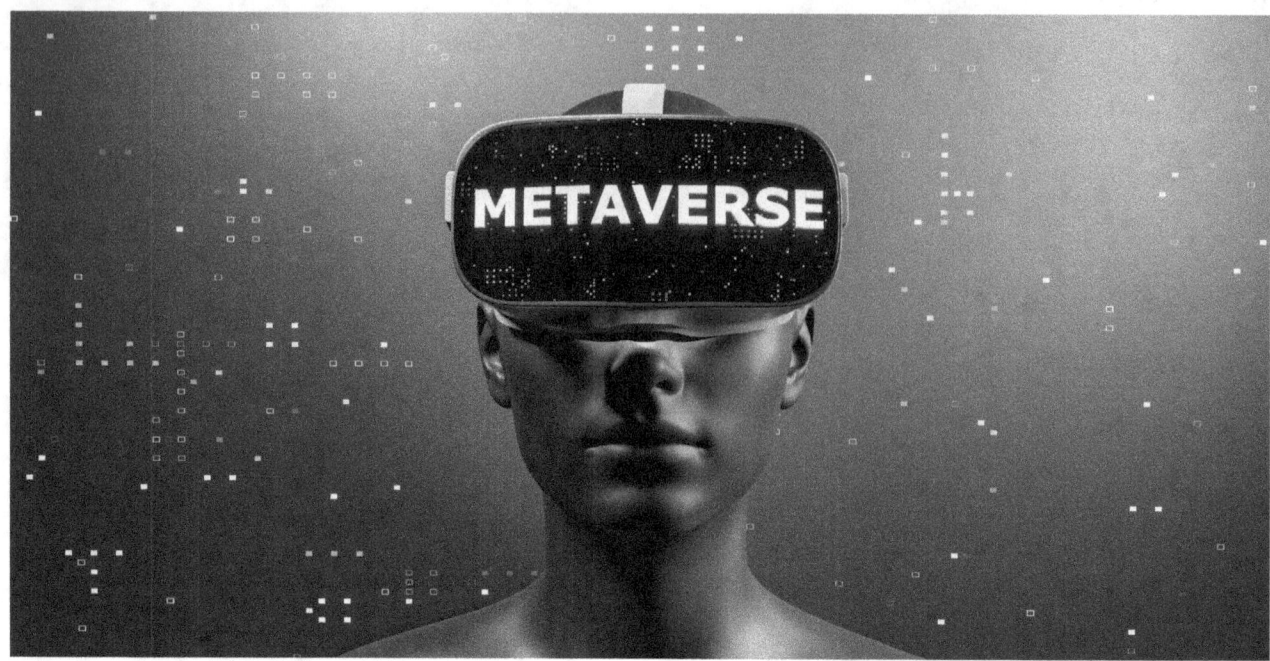

The Metaverses are here, representing the next stages in the Internet's growth. As a result, we will probably be able to access digital information through our smartphones or computers shortly, as those gadgets will become outdated. Yet, we will entirely be immersed in a virtual environment, capable of communicating with people from all over the world utilizing smart glasses.

Whether you love it or hate it, the market is coming, it will occur, and it will be priceless at $850 billion by 2030: When it comes to enterprises, what are the stocks of companies in which we may invest so as to benefit from the Metaverses' growth? Metaverses can be described in many different ways, but each definition boils down to exactly the same concept or idea: It has become the current worldwide hot topic.
The Metaverse is a collaborative VR environment that can be accessed through smart glasses and is completely interactive. Our connections will be multifaceted in this climate, just like they are today.

How do we now connect with one another? We interact on social media in two-dimensional or, at most, 3D worlds, similar to those in certain online games. But due to the Metaverse, we will have 4D interactions, allowing us to immerse ourselves in digital material rather than only viewing it.

When wearing virtual glasses and entering a virtual world, it is possible to dance with someone halfway across the world. To a great degree, it is similar to the Matrix, where we will surf in the desert or somewhere else. The Metaverse will change how we work, play, and learn in the future, and it will do so quickly.

The Metaverse is an emerging technology that allows us to travel virtually through the internet. Through glasses that connect directly to your brain, you can view 3D environments, meet other users and engage in many activities simultaneously. Imagine being able to go anywhere in the world instantly.

In addition, the Metaverse is also changing our interaction with video games. Through VR, you can experience the game from different points of view, and you can interact with others in ways that couldn't be done before.

Consider doing business meetings and interviews via a virtual office rather than via video chat or webcams. Consider putting on garments while sitting comfortably in your living room.

However, today's technological progress also poses a serious challenge to the existing order. The internet, social media, smartphones, and other technological advances have disrupted nearly every aspect of modern society.

We now live in an age where a vast majority of people are connected to each other through the internet. In fact, the average person spends almost two hours per day online. Some experts believe that this trend will continue to gain popularity.

In addition, the global population is rapidly aging. As a result, the demand for healthcare and retirement benefits are growing significantly.

It's becoming increasingly important for people to understand blockchain technology and cryptocurrencies like bitcoin. Blockchain and Bitcoin are changing the way companies operate, and the public views them.

But why do companies need blockchain? Why should I care about bitcoin? How does it work? Will I get rich? These questions and many others are answered by this book. You'll see how blockchain is revolutionizing everything from finance to social media. And if you're considering investing in altcoins or trading bitcoins, you'll discover the best exchanges and wallets to use.

What is the Metaverse?

The word 'metaverse' comes from a book written by Neal Stephenson called Snow Crash. In his book, Stephenson describes the Metaverse as an evolution of the internet. It is a virtual reality in which what happens in the Metaverse affects the real world. A metaverse is described as a digital ecosystem that's based on blockchain technology.

Technologies such as virtual reality (VR) and augmented reality (AR) are the visual component providers. The dispersed media makes it possible for continuous social engagement as well as economic opportunities.

These virtual worlds are interoperable, innovative, and adaptable, where they combine cutting-edge technology with interactive models within its members on an individual and organizational level.

Think of it like the Sims game, Roblox, or Fortnite. There are avatars, real estate, gaming, and lots of social interactions. It even has its own economy, where users can make money in a few different ways. You can sell land, rent out your land, create games that charge users to play, etc. The possibilities continue to grow.

Roblox was launched in 2006, and it 0quickly became America's favorite children's game. Half of the American kids under the age of sixteen were playing Roblox in 2020. In Roblox, users can create their games to make money. To play the games, players pay Robux, a virtual currency used by Roblox. The game creators can then exchange Robux for money.

Now, Roblox has decided to make its platform a step further to create a metaverse world that centers around its players.
The top competitor of Roblox is Fortnite. Fortnite, which was launched in 2017, has become popular as a social media space. The platform has even been able to put on virtual concerts with stars like Travis Scott and Ariana Grande.

Just like in these games, your metaverse avatar can walk around in virtual worlds, visit friends, attend events, check out auctions, and buy things.

In the Metaverse, there is a digital currency that is used to buy clothes, weapons, virtual real estate, and many other virtual items. Users can travel through the Metaverse virtually using a virtual reality headset and controllers.

Several companies developed online communities that were based on the concept of the metaverse, such as Second Life, which was released in 2003.

As of right now, the worlds of the Metaverse are still being created. The worlds that have been created are still separate but are meant to eventually come together as a new virtual reality universe.

These worlds would exist without you playing and some aspects of them are meant to be tied to the real world. A form of augmented reality combines the digital world with our world, making it possible for our real lives to intertwine with our virtual lives.
The idea that the users will be able to interact with one another just as they do in the real world is what the Metaverse seems to center around.

Mark Zuckerberg, the founder of Facebook and Instagram, describes it as a way to socialize as you would in the real world. In a sense, it is taking a video call a step further and adding video game aspects to it.

There has been some argument over whether the Metaverse is one entity or multiple entities, which are connected. Some have said it is like the universe, one entity made of several different worlds. Others refer to the virtual world, like Fortnite or Roblox, as a metaverse in and of its own.

Roblox and Fortnite were not the first ones to attempt this idea. In the early 2000s, a game called Second Life emerged. Interest and popularity in the idea of the Metaverse started to rise after the Global Pandemic, Covid 19, left people unable to interact with others in person. People everywhere flocked to the internet as a way to stay a part of the world and interact with one another.

Most people were forced to resume their jobs, school, and lives online. After being stuck inside for an extended period of time, the concept of being able to virtually travel to another world sparked the interest of both businesses and people alike.

This evolution of the internet takes cyberspace and expands upon the idea, creating a new way for us to interact with technology. Since the Metaverse is still being created, it is hard to define what it actually is. People come up with new ideas every day, so things can change quickly.

The core concept of the Metaverse is to create a virtual that mimics the real one, where anything you can do in reality is a possibility in the virtual world. Tech companies have started creating platforms to make the Metaverse a reality.

How Will It Work?

The Metaverse is divided into two kinds of platforms. The first platform leverages nonfungible tokens (NFT) and cryptocurrency to create blockchain-based Metaverse startups. Users can purchase real estate and create their own settings on Decentraland and the Sandbox platforms.

In these digital 3D universes, there are multiple processes and elements like communications, finances, game worlds, personal profiles, NFTs, and more.

The Metaverse's potential is attributed to the freedom it offers. At any given time, anyone in the Metaverse can create, purchase, and view NFTs to purchase virtual land, play games, develop virtual identities, and join social engagements. There is a vast range of use, and opportunities for monetizing real-world and digital assets, allowing enterprises as well as individuals to be able to integrate into the framework of the Metaverse. In the future, metaverses will join diverse online realms, with NFTs ensuring cross-chain interactions.

The second platform uses the term metaverse when describing virtual worlds. These are places that people can meet for personal or business reasons.

Virtual worlds are not only about building them but also about providing a platform for their users to interact with them. There are two main ways this happens: through the creation of a shared user experience and through the creation of a social network. A shared user experience means that all users see the same thing at the same time. For example, when you walk into a mall, you may notice that everyone in the store is wearing the same outfit or has the exact same hairstyle. This is what we call a "shared experience."

Some examples of shared experiences include the following:

1. Virtual worlds allow us to share our own personal experiences with others. We can invite friends to come to visit us in the Metaverse, or we can go visit them. If we choose to do the latter, we enter a shared virtual environment where we can meet up with our friends and explore together.

2. Shared experiences occur naturally in some virtual worlds. For example, if you play Minecraft, you might find yourself in a large open world where you can explore any part of the map without needing to ask anyone else for permission.

Blockchain-based platforms require the use of cryptocurrency to buy assets. Platforms like Decentraland and the Sandbox only accept Ethereum-based crypto tokens to buy or sell virtual property. Companies have started to look for ways that the Metaverse can work for them. Platforms like Fortnite and Roblox have created their own metaverse worlds, where users can interact with one another the way they would in real life. NFT avatars represent players, meaning NFT avatars can be used as access tokens to enter and travel between different sectors of the Metaverse. NFT avatars are used as an extension of our real-life identities in this situation. This allows us to combine and create virtual identities within the Metaverse.

In the Metaverse, a user's avatar is their virtual embodiment of them. It has the same legal authority in the Metaverse as a person's legal rights in the real world. That would mean that the avatar is respected for any transactions made within the virtual domain. It also restricts them from repudiating any committed action. Access can be gained by anyone who has a VR/AR-enabled immersive device, like a headset.

Microsoft HoloLens 2 is a Windows Mixed Reality device that runs Windows 10 and has an Intel Core i5 processor, 32GB RAM, and 128GB SSD storage. It has a dual 1440x1440 LCD display, an integrated 5-megapixel front camera, four microphones, Bluetooth connectivity, and WiGig wireless communication. It also supports both USB and Thunderbolt 3 ports for external hard drive and laptop connections.

Chapter 2: What Role Does Blockchain Play in the Metaverse?

In the future, there might be many different metaverses that you can visit. Each one might be controlled by a different company like Facebook, Microsoft, etc. However, none of those companies will allow you to visit all the others.

So we need a system to connect all these worlds together. And that's what blockchains do. Think of it as a giant database that everyone shares. Everyone stores information about their own version of reality in the database. These databases are called 'Blockchains'.

The Metaverse's economic system is composed of multiple virtual worlds, each with its currency. The idea is for the user to be able to travel seamlessly between worlds.
To do that, the user would have to have the currency for whichever world they travel to if they hope to buy assets or attend events. Cryptocurrency, digital tokens, and NFTs are the core of the metaverse economy. Each transaction made in the virtual world needs to have a record of it. Blockchain, which is considered a breakthrough technology when it comes to security and preserving privacy, laid the foundation for the existing digital currency market. It provides a system to record every transaction, like an enormous ledger, to protect both the buyer and seller.

These records of transactions are being stored as blocks, which are linked together using cryptographic measures, known as hashing mechanisms, to ensure the ledgers' immutability. Blockchain was designed as a way to keep records of the use and exchange of Bitcoin, a type of cryptocurrency. Its records can be accessed, some by permission and others without. Blockchain and cryptocurrency are the backbones of the metaverse ecosystems. Blockchain employs proof of work as the consensus mechanism. This method is more secure and better suited for e-commerce platforms.
In relation to the Metaverse, blockchain is the appropriate enabler to enforce accountability within the digital ecosystem.

The need for blockchain is imminent. The securing of digital content that is in possession of all users of the metaverse is its main purpose. The metaverse eco-system depends on blockchain for keeping track of their content and transactions to protect the users' integrity, privacy, and reputation.

Within the Metaverse, virtual clothing, digital property investment, homes, avatar accessories, and vehicles are going to be valuable. There are no limits as to what you are capable of doing in the Metaverse. If you can create noteworthy material and advertise it successfully, there is no stopping what you can do.

The Metonymy would even consider virtual careers, such as virtual real estate developers, Metaverse advisers, automobile and land leasing, and avatar architects, to name a few. Companies will need to focus their marketing strategies on a shared virtual economy and away from online advice.

The Metaverse has reimagined the concept of governing, in which multiple users work together to build and manage the Metaverse.
With the ability to buy and sell real estate and other goods, records will need to be kept to ensure the validity of each sale. With blockchain, a record of transactions, transferring of digital assets, and user-generated virtual locations.

Blockchain's transparent technology allows users security and freedom to be creative. Video games have been the cornerstone of the metaverse. The land is sold and rented for the creation of games.

The blockchain technology behind cryptocurrencies and decentralized apps is the foundation of the Metaverse. The ability to track transactions in real-time across multiple blockchains creates a shared ledger for tracking ownership of digital assets.

Blockchain is a distributed public database that keeps records of every transaction made within a system. The blockchain is secured using cryptography, making it impossible for anyone to alter any record without being detected. This security is what gives blockchain technology its trustworthiness.

By using smart contracts, blockchain technology enables programs to run automatically when certain conditions occur. Smart contracts are self-executing pieces of code that verify conditions and execute actions according to preprogrammed instructions, eliminating the need for third parties to oversee transactions.
The blockchain is immutable, meaning that once something is recorded onto the blockchain, it cannot be changed.

The blockchain metaverse needs a lot of open standards to facilitate interoperation among different types of media. For example, an app could render a movie using the WebGPU standard instead of the WebGL standard. Script compatibility is one of the key issues that need to be addressed.

There are many other aspects to consider when developing the standards. A few examples are: what kind of information should be stored in each block? How should the blocks be distributed across the network?

This is the point at which I realized that there were many different types of blockchains out there, and each had its own advantages and disadvantages.

Some blockchains could provide a transparent and secure record of ownership, while others could offer high throughput. There were also other factors to consider, including scalability, fees, security, and privacy.

Chapter 3: Top 5 Crypto Metaverse Projects

i. The Sandbox

The Sandbox is an Ethereum-based decentralized virtual world of the Metaverse and gaming. In it, you can create, share, and monetize games and assets. The Sandbox was designed as a way to give creators and gamers control over their inworld creations, unlike traditional gaming markets that allow platforms to own and control all user-generated content. Due to this, the rights of creators and gamers are limited.
There are three main aspects of The Sandbox. VoxEdit gives users the ability to create as well. as animate 3D people, animals, and other ASSETS of the metaverse. They allow both fungible and nonfungible tokens (NFTs) to be minted with a single smart contract with the use of the ERC-1155 token standard. The Sandbox Marketplace allows users to publish and sell their ASSETS after uploading them to the InterPlanetaryFileSystem (IPFS). Users can also create 3D games for free with The Sandbox game maker. Users can create, use, sell, and monetize NFTs, even with any tech knowledge.

$SAND is the Sandbox's virtual currency. 3,000,000,000 SAND will be in circulation. SAND can be bought or sold by third-party cryptocurrency exchanges like crypto.com, Kraken, and Gemini. Users can stake SAND through Uniswap (SAND/ETH) and mSAND/MATIC through Polygon for 36 percent to 113 percent APR.

SAND is used for all transactions in The Sandbox's marketplace. This includes buying LAND. The Sandbox LAND sales that are held on the map of The Sandbox website are the one place LAND in The Sandbox. Altogether, 166,464 LANDS will be available to purchase. An announcement about the dates of a sale will be made weeks in advance to give you time to prepare.

OpenSea and Rarible are third-party NFT exchanges where you can purchase land secondhand. These, however, are more expensive than purchasing LAND at an official sale.

After LAND is purchased, it will show up on your inventory on The Sandbox website, if the LAND is in the third-party wallet you signed up with.

LAND can be sold or rented out to creators in The Sandbox to use for their games. LAND owners will set their own rent. In the US, a piece of LAND started out costing around $593. Now a piece of LAND costs $4,773 (1.648 ETH).

The purpose of buying LAND is to be able to allow other users to host a variety of things, such as stores, games, and museums. Players will have to pay an entrance fee to be able to access the experience. The entrance fee will be paid in SAND.

Occasionally The Sandbox will hold events in which users can gain SAND tokens from playing games. They will also hold contests to allow users a chance to win SAND tokens. These events will be held on LANDs, in which the owners will profit from the paying players who want to participate in the event. LAND owners can also allow others to host events on their LAND as well as advertise on their LAND for a fee set by the owner.

Advertising your business is a great way to extend your reach to prospective consumers. Users can pay to advertise their services, goods, or businesses on other users' LAND.

ii. Decentraland Marketplace:

Decentraland is a 3D virtual world on the Ethereum blockchain. A parcel is a lot of land, or an NFT, that can be purchased at the Decentraland marketplace. If a player has two or more properties that are adjacent to each other, they can connect them and create an estate. This will save players the trouble of tending to a lot of different plots and focusing on one big plot. To turn plots into an estate, players will have to do it in the marketplace.

The Decentraland Marketplace is a one-stop-shop for everything related to land, estates, avatars, and other items needed to build a world. Trading in the Metaverse also takes place here. The Metaverse offers a way to purchase the property next to anyone they want to share a house with. For example, family members who live far apart or even celebrities could live with them.

You have the option to buy, sell, or rent in Decentraland. Land can be found in districts such as Crypto Valley, Fashion Street, Aetherian City, Vegas City, District X, etc.

The profits produced from those who use their land remain for the property owners. This is different from other systems in that they take a cut. Since the scheme is decentralized, there really isn't a centralized authority to govern it. This makes buying virtual land in Decentraland Metaverse a wonderful long-term investment.

You can play Decentraland for free but won't have access to all the features. The only services that are available for free in the world of Meta are exploring the Decentraland to find things you like, creating your customized Avatar, and interacting with other users. To access some of the most important features in the Decentraland, you'd need to purchase those features. To do this, you have to connect your account to your digital wallet. The decision to experience Decentraland without a wallet results in facing loss and missing out on many rewards and benefits.

Linking your Decentraland wallet will allow you to explore and make complete use of the platform. You can buy and accommodate your land with digital 3 Dimensional content and monetize the same for maximum benefit.

iii. Illuvium

Players explore the Illuvium landscape to battle Illuvials as well as other players, participate in quests and daily challenges. They can also participate in its communal storyline. During their journey, players collect Illuvials.

1. Illuvials

Illuvials are native beasts in the world Illuvium. Players will have to catch these creatures while they explore the world. Illuvials have different abilities and attacks, making each unique. Every one of these creatures is also an NFT that players can collect. This means that players can sell or trade them. After Illuvials are acquired, either by capture or purchase, they can be used inside the auto battler system. There they can fight in survival mode or choose between two arena modes.

2. Shards

Shards are among the most important items in the game. With these shards, players can capture Illuvials that they beat in combat. Players will want to be well-stocked with them before exploring the world.

You can get shards by mining them from deposits. Just make sure you have something on hand in case you encounter a rare Illuvial. Shards are classified by tiers based on their ability to capture Illuvial. The stronger the Illuvial, the more challenging they will be to capture. This is where you want to have a strong shard. The shard you pull from the ground could be of any quality. The most powerful ones will be the rarest. If you want to be able to capture every Illuvial you come across in the world, you will need an array of shards.

You will want to check out IlluviDEX, Illuviums NFT marketplace. That is where you can purchase shards. Players can also sell or trade Illuvials, NFTs, or farmed materials on the IlluviDEX.

There is a play-to-earn aspect of the game where players can earn ILV tokens through completing PVE quests, performing special achievements, and winning tournaments as well as events. Players can also participate in and wager on matches that are held in the Leviathan Arena. This is where players can battle one another to prove who is stronger.

3. Tokenomics

Illuvium's tokenomics is a breakdown of the distribution of $ILV 10,000,000 tokens and the revenue streams built into the game.

By using Balancer for their Launchpad, they were able to fairly distribute 1,000,000 tokens subject to no lockup enabling a healthy and stable price discovery process. The participants of the BLBP receive different promo NFTs for early purchasing, purchases of large quantities, or both. Rewards are also provided for participants who aren't able to outlay large amounts of capital through randomized NFT drops. This is where all the participants have entered automatically. That means that any and all participants have the chance to win rare NFTs.

The Illuvium Vault revenue streams are divided into two categories; In-game Purchases and IlluviDEX exchange fees.

In-Game Purchases include Shard Curing (used for catching Illuvials), Travel, Crafting, Cosmetics, Revival, and The IlluviDEX.

Exchange Fees as well as Wagering Fees are generated from every sale on the IlluviDEX at a starting rate of 5% of the total transaction value. The Immutable X platform (IMX) also takes a capped fee for every transaction on their network in exchange for waiving GAS fees. The primary in-game currency is ETH.

For the yield farming rewards, the fortnightly yield over time is a token Supply of 3,000,000. The yield update cycle is fortnightly at an adjustment ratio6, of 97%. Pool weights are initially $ILV/ETH: 0.8 and $ILV: 0.2

The Yield Pool contract is enabled to create "flash pools". These are temporary farming pools that are added by the eDAO for the purpose of distributing $ILV at a certain weight. This allows the flexibility to add new partners and to further distribute Illuvium tokens. All in-game purchases and fees in ETH are sent to the Vault contract. The Vault contract will periodically and automatically use the ETH to purchase an equal value of $ILV from the $ILV/ETH Uniswap V3 pool. The $ILV is then distributed to staked token holders in proportion to their stake.

Participants of both the $ILV / ETH as well as $ILV staking pools are given equal weighting for the purposes of Vault distributions.

As an incentive for long-term stakes, creators have developed an innovative distribution the system that differentiates between locked and unlocked tokens.
Stakers can opt to lock their staked tokens on a sliding scale for anywhere up to 12 months and gain a boost in their pool weight as a reward. The bonus is linear and has a maximum locking of 12 months; staked tokens are weighted as twice that of unlocked staked tokens.

Weighting will affect both Yield Farming Rewards as well as Vault Distributions. For those who choose to keep their staked tokens unlocked have the ability to withdraw them at any time.

Rewards have the option to be rolled over each distribution cycle. Stakers can claim when it's appropriate for them and avoid a high percentage of GAS fees. As a way to encourage participation and activity in the game, the ability to roll over is tied to in-game activity. To avoid having to make weekly claims, the linked account must be active for a minimum time period.

A portion of the in-game yield is distributed for tournament battles, quests, and daily challenges. This has been done in an effort to incentivize game-play as well as allow players who are lacking in capital to use sweat-equity to gain access to yield rewards.

$ILV rewards can be obtained through yield farming and are escrowed, where they are held by the vault for 12 months. During the 12 months, they can not be withdrawn. Stakers can forfeit those rewards and choose to claim an equal amount of $sILV, which is equivalent in value to $ILV. $sILV is the in-game currency. This allows the holder to spend their rewards earlier than the usual 12-month period. In-game purchases are indexed to USD. A price conversion from $sILV to USD, which is based on $ILV, is used. All tokens other than those bought in the BLBP and In-Game Yield are subject to a 12-month lockup period. After that, they are linearly unlocked over an additional 12 months. Tokens that were bought in the BLBP are unlocked, although a participant can choose to lock them and receive a higher distribution of $ILV in exchange for providing sustained liquidity for the in-game economy. All the tokens claimed through yield farming will also be locked and staked for 12 months.

The initial private and seed participants seem confident in the longevity of the protocol. The lockup period means that the majority of the tokens are going to be out of circulating supply. After studying the tokenomics of various successful protocols in the DeFi space, creators believe the mechanics in Illuvium will allow for a fair distribution of the $ILV token.

Risks are associated with DeFi, specifically staking and smart contract risk. Contract configurations are being developed constantly and are subject to change.

iv. StarAtlas

Star Atlas is considered the Metaverse's best and most innovative cryptography project. It is a gaming metaverse created with the foundations of multiplayer online games, real-time visuals as well as interactions, dispersed economic institutions, and blockchain technology. Star Atlas is on the Solana blockchain.

One of the main features of Star Atlas is asset exploration. Players scour the universe looking for assets. The resources discovered during the interstellar adventure can be minted, refined, and traded through the Star Atlas marketplace to make a profit. Players who aren't too excited about engaging in the combat aspect of the game can choose to continue with the adventure aspect of it.

While in the exploration mode, players can take control of the spaceship's controls, command their crews, and use other-worldly technology to find resources. A top-down view along with a first-person point of view of the cockpit, allows players to explore the uncharted areas of space in search of valuable resources.

In the future, players can install mining machinery to able to refine the resource in order to trade them in the marketplace and earn real-world money.
Users can acquire digital assets with the Star Atlas Metaverse, which includes equipment, territory, ships, and personnel.

Star Atlas has its own currency system called POLIS. It is primarily used to expedite the the game's many operations and services.
In an effort to address the lack of extensive gameplay, the Star Atlas team announced its next major browser gameplay module, ship configuration, resource extraction, and missions (SCREAM).

In SCORE, players are rewarded for enlisting their ships to their faction's fleet. In SCREAM, players will be rewarded in proportion to how much they earned for their factions through their actions.

There are also several interesting features and unique experiences in-store; Star Atlas has a good chance of quickly rising to the top of the Metaverse's cryptocurrency.

v. $UFO

UFO Gaming is a decentralized gaming platform with play-to-earn elements, NFTs, and DeFi functionality like staking, built on Ethereum. Its games, like Super Galactic, which is an RPG/arcade action game that has its own NFT collection and an auto battler, are integrated with Immutable X. Immutable X is a layer-two scaling solution for NFT projects on Ethereum.

In UFO Gaming there is a three-token system consisting of plasma points, UAP, and UFO. Creators claim that by using the game itself, NFTs, and a three-token system, they have created an internal economic loop that will ensure an infinite financial flow, as long as the game is popular.

$UFO is the primary token in UFO gaming. It connects everything in the ecosystem.

Players can mint UFOeps, playable characters in the form of NFTs. To do this, the player would need Plasma Points, the in-game utility points that can be farmed with UAP, the native UFO token.

With UFOeps, players battle a hostile alien race in a desolate world in order to defend the world while completing daily quests and earning rewards. UFOeps can be leveled up and sold on the UFO Gaming marketplace.

Future Predictions

Gov Capital predicts that UFO Gaming could increase by 45% within a year, reaching $0.0000115. DigitalCoinPrice's price prediction for 2022 is that it will average at $0.0000104,$0.0000118 in 2023, $0.0000158 in 2025, and in 2030 around $0.0000373. Price Prediction believes the token will average $0.00001048 in 2022, have an average price of $0.00003309 by 2025, and $0.000188 in 2030. Wallet Investor predicts the token will fall to $0.0000155 in a year's time.

Chapter 4: Metaverse Investments

To create the Metaverse, hundreds of stocks will need to be traded. Some of these will be necessary for the infrastructure of the Metaverse, while others will help the users of the Metaverse. These essential stocks will be classified into metaverse vital stocks.

Companies:-

i. Qualcomm

The communications chip company, Qualcomm, is branching outside of smartphone chipsets. One area of interest is the metaverse. Like AMD, Qualcomm has partnered with Meta Platforms.

It participates more in the forefront than AMD because it provides the semiconductors for the Oculus VR goggles. The company has also collaborated with Microsoft. Qualcomm will power Microsoft's AR glasses and Microsoft Mesh, which supports holographic images in a virtual setting.

In the first six months of fiscal 2022, which ended March 27, the revenue of $21.9 billion increased 5.9 % compared to the first six months of fiscal 2021. Their net income rose even faster during the period, increasing by 50% to over $6.3 billion as the company limited its cost and expense growth to 22%. Despite that increase, Qualcomm's stock is only up slightly on the year. The P/E ratio has dropped to 14, lower than every other major chip stock except for Intel. Considering the low multiple and the quick earnings growth, investors may want to buy this metaverse stock while it is still cheap.

ii. Meta Platforms Inc. (FB)

Founder Mark Zuckerberg changed the name of Facebook to Meta Platforms. This is due to the fact that he is absolutely convinced that the metaverse will be the evolution of the internet and social media.

The market, however, doesn't seem to share Zuckerberg's point of view. FB stock is down around 46% year to date through May 24. For now, Meta will continue to earn most of its money from Instagram and Facebook products. Investors believe that Meta's virtual reality plans are foolish. Although, Zuckerberg's previous capital allocation decisions, such as buying WhatsApp and Instagram, were highly successful. For those investors who are willing to bet on Zuckerberg once again, FB stock looks tempting at less than 16 times this year's projected earnings.

iii. Amazon

Amazon has announced its plans to enter the Metaverse and build a virtual economy. This will include virtual storefronts for users to visit. Cloud-based services are needed to create and manage Metaverse's architecture. Amazon Web Services is one of the most powerful players.

iv. Microsoft Corp. (MSFT)

Microsoft is one of the Big Tech powerhouses that has a significant metaverse angle. Microsoft has its HoloLens headset, primarily a business product. It sells for several thousand dollars and was created to assist with mixed-reality applications in settings like real estate, virtual communications, factories, and 3D printing. Eventually, Microsoft could be able to expand its virtual reality technology into its gaming division. Microsoft has already proven to be a leader in the console space. It should further broaden its gaming footprint with the help of its pending acquisition of Activision Blizzard Inc. (ATVI).

Content Creation Tools:-

i. Unity Software Inc. (U)

Unity Software is the developer of one of the two major video game engines, Unreal Engine being their biggest competition. Unity allows developers to produce top-quality graphical content, which runs across all platforms. This includes phones, laptops, consoles, and virtual reality. Unity has a projected 70% market share of

the mobile gaming market today. In the future, Unity will take its strong position in existing games and leverage it into success in the metaverse as well as other virtual platforms as well as augmented reality applications. Unity is also working on creating other purposes for its graphics software. Among them are video animation, architecture, and e-commerce. In the case of e-commerce, imagine 3D models of a person's body to make it easier to try on clothing and other accessories virtually so they can decide whether or not to buy them.

ii. Autodesk Inc. (ADSK)

The graphics software company, Autodesk, is already a large and strongly profitable company that has a metaverse angle to provide further upside potential for the stock. Autodesk's main product is software that provides advanced design tools to professionals. People, like architects, use Autodesk to design layouts for buildings, factories, skyscrapers, etc. The factory angle is exceptionally interesting since companies are beginning to use digital twins. This is a virtual re-creation of a physical object, like an assembly line of a factory. The engineers could experiment using virtual objects without the risk of damage to the real-world setup. With the success of enhanced-reality applications, companies like Autodesk that create the underlying modeling software will be positioned for further growth.

iii. Roblox Corp. (RBLX)

Roblox is one of the leading video game ecosystems. Roblox is not just a game. It is a platform in which users design their own games and content inside the Roblox universe. This has enabled Roblox to enjoy the strong network effects as users like hanging out and trying out one another's concepts. The primary limitations of Roblox are its weak graphics engine, as well as the fact that the majority of its consumers consist of children and teenagers. Investors have been skeptical of Roblox's long-term value if it is unable to reach a larger audience. Roblox has a vast community that should benefit from the metaverse. Brands have already started paying to set up their virtual advertising projects within the Roblox ecosystem. With Roblox shares down 74% year to date through May 24, Roblox shares have dropped enough to have become tempting to the more risk-tolerant investors.

iv. Disney

Disney is indeed the item in the Metaverse stock market. You may think Disney has nothing to do with Metaverse technology, but that would be wrong. You would be missing out on the point that a company does not have to be tech-savvy to be relevant in the Metaverse. Intellectual property is as important as physical property, and whether it comes to royalties, Disney is a master.

Disney owns properties like the Marvel and Star Wars movies. It will be left to the Metaverse to incorporate the world's top franchises when the time comes, and the price will be set by the Disney corporation. As a bonus, don't forget about Disneyland, which will eventually become the most popular virtual destination.

With or without the Metaverse, Disney's shares are an excellent investment because they provide consistent profits to shareholders. Disney shares, however, have the potential to grow if acquired today and kept over a long time. Don't wait until massive changes to movie theaters happen before you buy Disney shares.

The film industry is one of the most technically advanced, and 3D movies have become increasingly common. It'll just be a matter of time before movie theaters implement mixed and VR technology to create a more immersive experience.

Semiconductors:-

i. NVIDIA

NVidia is the leading company, with AMD being a close second. NVidia is responsible for hardware development. The chip is made by the Taiwan semiconductor manufacturing business. TSMC provides 90% of these high-end sophisticated chips that have a diameter of fewer than five nanometers.

NVIDIA is a market leader when it comes to Gaming, Data Center Computing, Visualization, and Automotive Technologies. NVIDIA is at the forefront of high-performance Graphics Cards or (Graphical Processing Units, GPUs). The global graphics processing unit (GPU) market was worth $22 billion in 2020 and had a projected Compounded Annual Growth Rate (CAGR) of 31.87% till 2028, reaching a market value of $165 billion.

ii. *Advanced Micro Devices*

AMD is a leading designer of GPUs and GCPUs that focuses on the video gaming and data center sectors. The recent acquisition of Xilinx elevated AMD's supercomputing capabilities while adding a radio frequency identity (RFID) chip to its already impressive portfolio. Offerings like these caught the attention of Meta Platforms. The Facebook parent announced last year that its data center would be run by AMD's EPYC processors. AMD continues to take market share from its longtime rival, Intel. According to Mercury Research, as of now, AMD claims a record 28% market share in the processor market.

The recent purchase of Pensando will also enhance the company's data center and edge computing capabilities. AMD's financials reflect these successes. During the first quarter of 2022, which ended March 26, AMD's revenue of $5.9 billion had increased 71% compared to year-ago levels. The $1.6 billion in non-GAAP net income AMD earned during the quarter rose 42% compared to the same quarter last year. However, high operating expenses and a $293 million amortization charge on acquisition-related intangible assets affected profitability.

Even with the declines in the recent months, the company's stock price rose by 35% in the last year. That increase took its P/E ratio to 40, significantly lower than the 53 earnings multiple of their rival Nvidia. This makes it a wonderful option for investors who would like to invest in this part of the Metaverse but think that Nvidia is too expensive.

Chapter 5: Where to Invest

i. Stocks

Buying "metaverse stocks" is one of the methods that people who are interested in the Metaverse might invest in. Holdings in publicly listed companies that are participating in the development of the metaverse are known as metaverse stocks. A good example of metaverse stocks is Facebook. It is a company you may want to buy if you want to invest in the metaverse.

Facebook's CEO, Mark Zuckerberg, has stated that he doesn't want the company to be seen as a social media company. He wants it to be recognized as a metaverse firm instead.

If you don't want to invest in Facebook, the social media company already has an Oculus virtual reality headset and has recently introduced its first smart glasses in collaboration with Ray-Ban augmented reality in an effort to expand its AR platform. Other businesses like Microsoft, Roblox, Unity Software, Amazon, Walt Disney, and Nvidia hope to play a part in the metaverse's evolution.

ii. Land and Property

The term land refers to real estate, but also virtual land. A land is a form of property that has been defined by law. The land is usually owned by governments, corporations, or private individuals. The land is often associated with real estate, which includes buildings, houses, and other structures built on the land. The land is also sometimes referred to as reality.

Virtual land is a type of virtual property that exists only in a computer program. It is created through the use of blockchain technology. A virtual land is a form of digital asset that can be bought and sold just like physical land. Some examples of virtual land include Minecraft, Second Life, and World of Warcraft.

How does one acquire land in a virtual world? Well, one does not actually own the land because it is owned by others but rather has a claim to the land. One can purchase pixels that represent the land and ownership rights within the sandbox metaverse. These pixels can then be clicked on to access the metaverse and purchase land. Once purchased, the pixel representing the land is displayed on the map of the sandbox metaverse and can be interacted with. The land can be sold back to the original owner after a certain amount of time.

Purchasing land is also a great way to invest in the Metaverse. It requires the same purchasing conditions as crypto. When the user has a digital wallet in place, they are able to select an emerging metaverse platform, explore the layout as well as available parcels, find the parcel they want, and make a purchase.

The process is pretty straightforward, but it involves more risk than pure-play crypto token investments since the value of virtual land will depend on a number of factors, like the pace of developing adjacent parcels. It is, however, among the most popular methods of investment. Analysts predict the market could reach $1 billion USD this year. You would be surprised how much some of this land is selling for if you understood its true value. We may acquire land in the sandbox metaverses by clicking on the buy property button. This then will redirect you to a platform where others may purchase NFTs, other forms of digital assets, and even physical items. We may look at them, realizing how expensive some of these areas are. It is an insane situation.

According to the recently listed part, lawful land is priced between 1.5 and two Ethereum, depending on the region's theme. That is probably valued somewhere in the market for $4500. The cost of land can range from about $900 to $10,000 for a few graphics on a computer screen. Once you've bought the property, it will display on the map, alongside different icons denoting those who possess the land in the sandbox metaverse.

Another game developer has also acquired sandbox metaverse property. Many individuals and potential businesses may be found in their hundreds around the metaverse who have acquired land there. You may wonder how investing in this land, and acquiring land inside these metaverses constitutes an economic opportunity. As previously stated, as the number of users utilizing this Metaverse and its coins rises, the amount of land available for purchase becomes progressively constrained by the excessive need. At this point, the concept of supply versus demand is well defined. Due to a limited source, individuals can demand any value they'd like to sell their land for. If you're thinking you might be a somewhat shrewd landowner and investor in these metaverses, then you must explore some of the markets available on these various metaverse marketplaces to find some of the things you could find.

Tokens:-

One of the easiest ways to invest in the metaverse involves the purchase of metaverse tokens, cryptocurrency. Buying tokens is easy to do. You will need a digital wallet to hold your crypto tokens as well as to be able to participate in a coin exchange. Choose the metaverse platform you would like to invest in and buy tokens for that virtual world. These are the most popular tokens right now.

i. ApeCoin (APE)

APE is an ERC-20 token; it exists on the Ethereum blockchain. It is considered a governance and utility token, which enables users to participate in the governing of the Ape ecosystem. This also provides them access to games, various products as well as services only available to ape coin holders.

It is expected that soon ApeCoin holders are going to be able to use their coins in an upcoming metaverse game from Yuga Labs, Otherside. Yuba Labs recently made around $320 million in a virtual land sale which allowed APE token holders to buy land parcels in Otherside. Ape holders bought 55,000 lots, known as 'Otherdeeds,' and 45,000 went to other individuals, such as the owners and project developers of Yuba Labs NFT. The traffic caused by the sale increased the Ethereum network's "gas fees," which is the fee each player pays to participate in a transaction over Ethereum, and eventually crashed the blockchain.

ApeCoin was launched on March 17(—a projected 30% of the maximum supply of 1 billion coins was expected to be in circulation. Despite being such a new token, Apecoin already has a market cap of $4.38 billion, which makes it the most-valued metaverse coin.

ii. MANA

Decentraland (MANA), which was launched in February 2020, is the second-most valued Metaverse project. It is the most popular Metaverse, having the most users, which makes it a must-watch in 2022.

Decentraland is one crypto metaverse project that has grown in popularity. This was partly due to the NFT craze, which has also led to dramatic gains for the platform's native tokens, MANA.

MANA is a Polygon-compatible ERC-20 token on Ethereum's blockchain. MANA is used to claim rewards, buy wearable NFTs in Decentraland, participate in exclusive activities and events, etc.

Decentraland (MANA) also features a growing virtual real estate marketplace similar to The Sandbox. Users are able to buy land for around $7k, allowing them to monetize it or create unique designs with ease.

iii. Axie Infinity (AXS)

Axie Infinity (AXS), which launched in 2018, is one of the pioneers of the play-to-earn Metaverse as well as NFT-based games. It was one of the first games to allow players a chance to earn a significant income from playing the game.
Axie Infinity has one of the most active NFT marketplaces. It's also one of the largest Metaverse crypto games are on the market as of right.

In Axie Infinity, the gameplay centers around players trying to collect monster NFTs called Axies. Players can use their Axies to battle, take on quests, and earn rewards.

Players also have the ability to upgrade their Axies, as well as breed/, evolve them into a more powerful version.

Axie Infinity also has the benefit of being very affordable. Players can buy an Axie for under $20 and immediately start playing the game. AXS might be a great opportunity to take advantage of while the price is low.

The game has a dual token ecosystem that includes the SLP utility and AXS governance assets. SLP allows players to breed/upgrade Axies. AXS enables users to buy Axies from the marketplace as well as participate in DAO governance. You can buy AXS on FTX, KuCoin, Binance, Gemini, Kraken, etc.

iv. NFTs and Wearables

Pixel art or GIF graphics might have been auctioned for millions of dollars using a mechanism called NFT. An NFT is designed to keep track of a specific piece of digital art. The creator of the artwork establishes that they are the owners and creators of the art.

The NFT is stored on a blockchain, which can be used to prove ownership. This will ensure that the artist gets paid whenever their artwork is used. The artist could sell their royalty by exchanging quasi tokens for cash, other NFTs, or cryptocurrency. NFTs will soon branch out into other areas like music, sports, entertainment, etc. As people transfer their trade in their tangible possessions for digital ones, NFTs will become more essential.

NFTs will play a vital role in the community, identification, and social experiences in Metaverse. Users can show support for or opinions on a project in the virtual and real-world by holding particular NFT assets. This enables people with similar NFTs to create groups, share their experiences, and develop content together.

Avatar NFTs grant virtual membership to different unique Metaverse and real-world activities, which promotes community along with social interactions. NFT avatars contribute to defining the metaverses' experiences and environments through launching startups and content creation.

The play-to-earn gaming concept captures the attention of and empowers blockchain game participants. Players can take part in the in-game economies of the Metaverse as well as receive incentives for the value they offer by depending on NFTs, allowing them to earn while they play.

In 2021, the market for NFTs rose by an outstanding 1785 percent. The spike in NFTs token usage raises the value of digital assets. This is piquing the interest of the virtual economy.

Wearables are becoming an important part of our lives. You can already get notifications when your friends come online, see what your favorite team is doing, and even watch movies on your wrist.

We've seen a lot of innovation in the past few years, but it seems like the industry is ready to go mainstream. While there are still many challenges with VR, AR, and MR technology, we're starting to see the first real products hit the market. Some of them are great, while others aren't quite ready for prime time. But the fact remains that the consumer market is about to explode.

The RealWear HMT-0 is a wearable device designed specifically for industrial workers such as warehouse staff. It connects to your smartphone via Bluetooth, allowing you to receive real-time messages about incoming shipments or inventory levels. The device also allows you to view the status of each shipment, making it easier for you to quickly locate items when needed.

Potential Markets in the Metaverse:-

Metaverse is a decentralized digital platform for creating and sharing virtual worlds. Anyone can create their own virtual universe and share it with others. While the technology behind the platform is still evolving, the basic concept of the metaverse already exists.

In fact, there are several companies already working on ways to incorporate technology into everyday life. For example, we already have Google Glasses that allow us to see our real-life surroundings while also seeing what we're looking at through augmented reality.

We also have Oculus Rift, a virtual reality headset, and HTC Vive, a virtual reality system. These technologies could be incorporated into the metaverse in the near future

i. Virtual Goods

Virtual goods are an emerging industry that allows users to buy and sell items that only exist in the online space. These items can range from clothing, accessories, and even furniture. Brands like Nike and Adidas have already begun selling merchandise through platforms like Roblox and Minecraft.

Real-life garments made with a digital backend, digital fashion rendered onto physical representations of people in real-life, and direct-to-avatar, the latter of which is exclusive to the Metaverse. Digital fashion is currently one of the fastest-growing sectors of the fashion industry. Virtual reality is already used to sell fashion items and brands in the form of filters, skins, and avatars.

Augmented reality is also very promising because it allows us to see our own avatar wearing clothes that we could not otherwise wear. The Metaverse is the perfect platform for this type of fashion because it provides a safe space for people to purchase and consume fashion without any risk of negative consequences.

The rise of digital fashion has been driven by the increasing popularity of augmented the reality, virtual reality, and blockchain technology.

These technologies allow us to create our own avatars and customize them to fit our preferences. In addition, we can buy and sell these avatars as collectibles via cryptocurrency. Users can also purchase NFTs that represent the item itself. These NFTs can then be stored on a blockchain ledger and traded between users. This allows people to trade their avatars and NFTs for other items.

Digital fashion is not only about owning an item but also about having ownership of your avatar. As a result, many brands are now launching their own NFTs. Some of the most notable examples include Bored Apes Yachts Club, which launched its first NFT in 2019. It represents one of the members of the club.

Virtual shopping is becoming increasingly popular as a way to buy goods online. It allows you to browse through thousands of items without leaving your house. You can also chat while browsing and even meet people from all over the world. Many companies are starting to offer services like those offered by Redfox Labs. These companies allow users to create their own virtual stores and sell their products to other customers. Some of them even let you create special promotions and discounts. For example, if you are running a fashion brand, you might want to give away free shirts to customers who follow your social media account.

ii. Digital Art

Artists can create their own virtual galleries in all the major worlds like Decentraland and CryptoVoxels. These worlds allow artists to showcase and sell their creations while interacting with potential buyers. Digital artists can open their own virtual galleries in these worlds and invite others to visit them through voice chat. The Metaverse allows artists to build a community and hold events. This is one reason why the popular BoredApeYachtClubNFT art project is making investments to purchase land and host events within the decentralized platforms. This includes creating a club on land purchased in the sandbox, with admission reserved for owners of the BoredApeNFT token. The world's oldest auction house, Sotheby's, has created a digital replica of their real-world venue in London.

iii. Virtual Real Estate

Virtual real estate, as discussed previously, has enormous commercial potential within the Metaverse. Similar to website domain names, virtual land will serve as the digital ground for virtual shopping malls, retail strips, casino districts, and many other lucrative business models.

For virtual property developers, there is an economic incentive and commercial benefit of locking up interconnecting plots of virtual land called estates or districts, which allow them to create unique value and build upon an existing community.

By owning plots of virtual land adjacent to each other, they can create districts founded around an interest or common theme and drive targeted users to their location on the map. Sports districts, for example, could be populated with virtual sports arenas, gaming, social meetup, music concerts, and live performances. In regards to sports, a designated area could offer a place to play virtual sports or watch.

iv. Online Gaming

One of the most exciting aspects of blockchain technology today is its potential to disrupt the industry of online gaming. These platforms allow anyone to easily launch a game, regardless of technical knowledge. Moreover, if the game is successful, the developer earns profits through micro-transactions and other sources of revenue.

In addition, because these games are not controlled by a centralized entity, they are immune to censorship and regulation. However, there are downsides to operating a game on a decentralized network. For example, latency is higher due to the fact that transactions must be processed via smart contracts; while this may seem like a minor issue at first, it becomes a problem when dealing with large numbers of concurrent users. Another downside is that the games themselves cannot be stored on a central server. Instead, they must be downloaded to each individual player's device, thereby limiting scalability.

Additionally, since the games are distributed across several devices, the possibility exists of data loss. Lastly, some players may not be willing to download a client that requires them to store personal information on third-party servers. Overall, the benefits of running a game on a decentralizing platform outweigh any drawbacks.

Ethereum into Brazilian Real (BRL) at a rate determined by the current market price. If they wanted to keep the BRL, they could exchange it back for ETH. However, if they did not want to hold any cryptocurrency, they could simply cash out their ETH directly into USD. The experiment was short-lived, lasting only two months.

v. Construction

With the rise of digital fabrication tools, an industry of virtual architects, vase designers, and builders has emerged. These professionals create complex structures using software like Unity or Unreal Engine 4, which allows them to design their own assets. Many virtual service providers exist online, offering custom designs for private islands, hotels, casinos, and even virtual cities.

While many of these companies offer free plans, some charge a monthly subscription fee to access more advanced features. Virtual construction ideas may also inspire actual construction, with players using 3d printers to replicate structures from the virtual world in reality.

vi. Virtual Events

The metaverse is an online world that allows users to create their own 3D virtual spaces. They can buy virtual items like furniture and clothing and decorate them according to their preferences. They can also attend social events and parties. There are many different types of events happening in the metaverse.

Some of the most popular ones include music concerts, art exhibits, fashion shows, workshops, language lessons, and after-parties. Virtual weddings are becoming increasingly popular. These events usually involve marriage counseling, and the participants get to choose their own names and personalities. For example, you can become a high roller at a casino in Second Life. You can play games, gamble, win prizes, and eventually, quit if you lose all your money. In Second Life, there are also sports teams. People can sign up to be players on any team that they wish.

Chapter 6: Investing Truth: Venture Capital

The reality is that a majority of investors won't be a good fit for Metaverse investing. Metaverse technology is rather obscure, and the business is still developing. Investors want a normal return, meaning a return on their investment within five years. If you're just entering the start-up world, this means that when investors donate money to a start-up in exchange for equity or partial ownership, they expect the company to be purchased or to go public in around five years.

Companies these days only have a few IPOs every five years, if any. In five years, they expect you to be acquired or purchased. That is just not a realistic expectation for the majority of Metaverse businesses today.

Investors need to be in it for the long haul. Not everyone is capable of doing that. The firms that bring the most value to the Metaverse will become those that are developing behind-the-scenes goods. Since these goods are not always easy to understand, the mix of a long return on investment term and hot firms makes it hard to envision products. It also complicates the link between venture capital and the Metaverse. It is only right for a certain type of investor.

How the Metaverse Will Replace Traditional Tech:-

The Metaverse will be molded by the technology in which we use to access it. This could include virtual reality (VR), augmented reality (AR), as well as brain-computer interfaces (BCI). The major technology companies, which include Apple, Google, Niantic, Meta Platforms (Facebook), Microsoft, and Valve, are creating the tech that will shape the future of the Metaverse.

The Metaverse will revolutionize almost all aspects of life and business within the next decade. This allows collaboration in virtual spaces, augmented physical places as well as a blend of the two. It will create new lines of business while transforming interactions between companies and customers.

Answering questions regarding how the Metaverse might look and feel, instead of wondering about its features may prove to be a useful viewpoint to predict the wave of socioeconomic change that the Metaverse will unleash.

If technologists are correct that 2022 will separate the thinkers from the builders, then the technical advances of last year will produce this year's first steps towards turning the Metaverse into a reality. Progress will be attributed to the always improving graphics processing units (GPUs), photorealistic 3D engines, faster content generation via volumetric video and artificial intelligence, the continuing popularity of cloud computing, and 5G, as well as a more sophisticated and better-understood blockchain infrastructure.

From the perspective of the human experience, one development stands out above all others. That is extended reality (XR) technologies, including virtual reality (VR), augmented reality (AR), as well as brain-computer interfaces (BCI), which together position themselves as the next computing platforms.

XR has made progress toward mainstream adoption. There are predictions that VR and AR headsets will surpass global game console shipments in 2024. Just like the introduction of the personal computer and smartphones before them, vast consumer adoption of XR headsets is anticipated to revolutionize human digital experiences. It is likely to offer the entry points of choice to the Metaverse.

The question of which XR technology ultimately wins is the subject of tense boardroom discussions, corporate chess board moves, and rising investment activity.

In today's Metaverse, virtual reality is the "digital escape." In the next few years, the Metaverse is expected to manifest itself mainly through virtual reality, which is an alternative, the digital world can be used for various personal and enterprise purposes. High-profile announcements by Meta Platforms (formerly Facebook), Microsoft, and Sony, all suggest that headsets like Meta Quest or Sony PSVR are going to be the consumer choices in which to navigate the interactive and social 3D environments.

Virtual reality is focused on developing a digital presence, which experts agree will be the key to developing an engaging experience and retaining users. Mark Zuckerberg claims that the metaverse, in the form of popular video games, is already here. Tech experts expect to see Meta acquire a major gaming franchise in 2022, following Microsoft's $68.7 billion acquisition of Activision Blizzard and Sony's $3.6 billion purchase of Bungie. The company's Oculus app, which will soon be rebranded as Meta Quest, was leading the app store this holiday season, during which Meta might have sold around two million VR headsets.

The advent of affordable virtual reality (VR) headsets have created a new industry, enabling users to interact with virtual worlds and experience new types of media. Virtual reality is a type of immersive experience that immerses users in interactive computer-generated environments.

Unlike other forms of entertainment like movies or television, VR creates a completely simulated environment. Users wear a headset that displays images to their eyes that appear to come from within the simulation. Headset manufacturers have been able to lower the price of VR equipment significantly since 2016, allowing consumers to purchase a basic headset for less than $200. Some models can also display stereoscopic images, giving users the perception of depth.

Let's look at the differences between these two technologies. Virtual reality requires a headset with goggles and headphones in order to completely immerse yourself in a fake environment.

AR involves the overlay of information on your normal perception of the world, like Google Glass. Both require advanced head-mounted display (HMD) systems, but unlike VR, there aren't any physical barriers blocking out natural light around the user. Some critics say that HMDs isolate people and make them look unattractive.

Many types of eyewear naturally make people look different when worn by others. In the near future, we can expect augmented realities to become more prevalent than virtual realities because they don't need any special equipment or software. This is partly due to AR's lighter method of interaction (assessed through a smartphone and not large earphones). Also, it can be applied to any type of application (not just games) that we see today on our phones or tablets.

The first commercial version of Google Glass was launched in 2013 as an Explorer edition. Other companies have also followed suit with similar products. These include Sony's SmartEyeglass and Microsoft's HoloLens.

Virtual Reality and Augmented Reality are two technologies that are currently starting to take hold. These technologies could eventually replace all aspects of our lives. We'll see them in movie theaters, on TV, at sporting events, and even inside our homes. Both of these technologies require special hardware.

For example, you need a headset to view virtual reality and a pair of glasses to wear augmented reality. As technology continues to advance, we'll likely see many more forms of immersive media come into existence, including holographic projections, wireless brain interfaces, and even full-immersion virtual reality.

Currently, most virtual environments are created under proprietary systems, so users who move between them need to learn new interfaces each time. Thus, to push the idea into mainstream use, we need to create an open-source system or body of standards.

It's important to note though, that even if we did get a standard interface in, one problem would be peoples' natural resistance to change. People may not want to abandon their existing virtual world for whatever reason, whether it's based on an old standard, or because they've built a huge following there over time. We see this with chat tools, where people still use IRC chat despite being replaced by newer online tools for interacting socially.

One possible way around the problem would be to keep and maintain both types of worlds around. Similar to what we see today with Second Life, where users can log into both the old SL grid and the new OpenSim grid. Few projects are currently pursuing this idea, but it's an exciting concept that could help solve the transition problem if implemented properly.

The ability of users and developers alike to access their assets and records across all virtual worlds is also critical to the long-term success of a thriving virtual world. In traditional games, users accumulate rewards, rankings, and other assets in a single game, but then start from scratch when they switch to a new game.

Businesses are racing toward a future that is vastly different from the one they were designed to operate in. In the near future, every company will find itself at the crossroads of various new worlds, from developing new physical and virtual realities to providing services in environments that were created by others.

To be able to grow and thrive in this new and quick-changing world, the strategies that organizations created now must have responsibility at their center, from ownership of data, to inclusion and diversity, sustainability, personal safety, and security.

How to Invest

i. ETFs

The easiest way to invest in the Metaverse is through an exchange-traded fund or ETF. ETFs are diversified, reducing volatility, which lowers risk exposure in the market. Currently, investors can invest in the Roundhill Ball Metaverse ETF (META) fund through your brokerage account. It is the oldest and largest fund to date. It focuses on companies in gaming, IAAS (Infrastructure as a Service), and the computer hardware space.

ii. Global X FinTech ETF (NASDAQ:FINX)

Global X FinTech ETF (NASDAQ:FINX) usually follows the Indxx Global FinTech Thematic Index, leading holding companies in the financial technology sector. The underlying companies seek to digitally remaster mature industries such as fundraising, insurance as well as third-party lending. Close to 78% of holdings in Global X FinTech ETF (NASDAQ:FINX) are centered in the information technology sector, and 14% are concentrated in the financial industry.

iii. Roundhill Ball Metaverse ETF (NYSEARCA: METV)

The Roundhill Ball ETF invests in 40 companies that are actively involved in creating the Metaverse. Nearly 80% of its holdings are based in the United States, and the remaining 20% come from Asia.

METV invests in the world's largest technology companies, such as Microsoft and Apple. METV's two biggest holdings are Nvidia and Roblox. Nvidia, a chip manufacturer, helps to build the infrastructure that is vital to the metaverse. Roblox, a gaming company, is responsible for the development of virtual worlds.

This was the first Metaverse ETF to be launched. It entered the market in June 2021 and remains the most popular Metaverse ETF. It contains a number of large-cap and stable companies, meaning it provides a safe way to invest in this upcoming trend.

iv. Evolve Metaverse ETF (TSX: MESH)

MESH, Canada's first metaverse ETF, provides investors access to an actively managed, diversified portfolio of companies that are involved in the creation of the metaverse. MESH consists of companies from around the world, particularly the United States and Asia.

Roughly three-quarters of the fund belongs to American companies. The remainder is made up of Chinese, Japanese, and Singaporean businesses. MESH mainly invests in the technology sector. This includes some of the best-known large-cap stocks such as Meta, Autodesk, and Walt Disney.

Since MESH is a relatively new ETF, there isn't much information on its historical movements. It currently has over $8m under management. MESH's biggest draw is its equal weighting. It divides its total fund among all of the stocks it invests in. This means that no single company can significantly affect its performance.

v. Stocks

You can get shares in a lot of different public companies in the Metaverse. One of them is a big player in the platform. You should be aware that there are publicly traded corporations such as Nvidia, Broadcom, Qualcomm, and Unity Technologies.

There are also behind-the-scenes businesses that help the Metaverse operate. These are places where you can make money. If you're looking for an investment opportunity, this is the place to go. This includes content creators who are making movies and TV shows. We think you'd be interested in what they're doing. In our opinion, this also covers streaming services like Netflix, Disney, Hulu, and Amazon. We'll only consider investments in publicly traded corporations, leaving private businesses and startups out. You can't invest in these firms unless you're a member of the venture capitalist community.

Anybody may invest in some alternative ventures such as Republic, beginning engines, and a number of other crowdfunding platforms. One way to invest in this organization involves devoting your time to studying how technology works.

vi. Fastly

Cloud computing has become a reality, and it's a great thing. However, there is a downside to this method of processing information. Data needs to travel through various networks before it reaches its destination. While this is not a big deal for simple searches like "what is the weather like today?" it becomes a problem when you are trying to access something like healthcare data.

Healthcare providers need real-time data to operate, but it takes days for data to get to them. This delay can cause problems for patients who need timely results. To solve this issue, companies like Fastly have come about. These companies provide services that help reduce the amount of data traveling from the source to the destination.

One example of this is that they move servers and routers close to the originator of the data. The data travels a shorter path and arrives quicker.

vii. Shopify

One of the most important aspects of the Metaverse is that it wants to become the first fully functioning Virtual World Economy. To accomplish this goal, the Metaverse needs assets, money, and a way to compensate content creators. These three components will allow the Metaverse to thrive.

Shopify has taken two significant steps toward the creation of a Metaverse economy. First, the company acquired an augmented reality app called Primer. 8Second, Shopify introduced a new platform for selling non-fungible tokens. These two moves connect Shopify to the emerging Metaverse economy.

viii. Google

Google is a fascinating company to invest in because of its exposure to data and AI potential. Google has always had a strong focus on technology, especially search and advertising. It has made many acquisitions and investments related to these areas. But in 2015, Google restructured into two separate companies, Alphabet Inc. and Google LLC. This separation allowed Google to pursue new ventures without distracting from its core businesses.

One such venture is Google X, formerly called X Labs. Here, Google has launched hundreds of different moonshot projects, including self-driving cars and high-tech contact lenses.

These projects may seem far-fetched today, but Google's interest in virtual and augmented reality is only a hint at what lies ahead.

Google's interest in virtual reality (VR) and augmented reality (AR) is only the tip of its iceberg. If we consider Google's interest in autonomy, it is clearly visible that the company is advancing at a pace unseen before in history.

The firm is undoubtedly one of the most advanced in terms of both autonomous driving technology and deep learning. DeepMind, a subsidiary of Google, recently developed an AI system is capable of predicting the 3D structure of proteins based on their amino acid sequences. Such knowledge could pave the way toward more efficient drug design.

Google opted to make this information publicly available to accelerate life science research. However, do not forget about Google itself. Data, entertainment, connectivity, and the search will define the next stage of the Internet. For years,' Google' and "Internet" have become synonymous terms. Given Google's own vision,
AI skills, on-the-ground deployment, and data gathering capabilities, it is hard to imagine the existence of the Metaverse without Google contributing substantially.

ix. Invest Successfully

Successful investors must be aware of four factors. They include the following. First, you must be knowledgeable about the products you are buying. Second, you must understand the optimal timing for purchasing the stock. Third, you must be informed of the proper quantity of shares to purchase, and fourth, you must be able to choose the right time to sell and collect your profits.

Most people fail because they lack knowledge of the products they are trading. They purchase a stock at the wrong time, overvalue it, or overprice it. As a result, they lose money. Some people fail because they cannot properly time their trades. They enter a stock prematurely before it has been retracted to a support level, or they wait until after it has been retracted.

Others fail because they do not know how to select the correct quantity of shares to purchase or when to sell. Finally, many people fail because they do not understand the fundamentals behind a particular stock. They buy a stock because it looks good, even though it does not meet the requirements of being a great investment. In conclusion, successful investing requires more than just knowing what to buy. Successful investors must be knowledgeable about the various products they are trading.

Then, they must understand the optimal timing of purchases. Lastly, they must be informed of the correct quantity of shares they should purchase, and they must be able to choose a time to sell and collect their profits.

In the early days of the internet, there were many ways to create content. You could write articles, create podcasts, record videos, etc. As time went on, platforms became more specialized.

Today, we have apps, websites, and social media platforms. Each of them has its own unique strengths and weaknesses. For example, an app might be great for creating short videos, while a website might be best for long-form content. If you can create content for multiple platforms, you will be well-positioned to capitalize on any changes in the market.

You can buy shares in a handful of publicly traded corporations in the Metaverse. You should be aware that there are publicly traded corporations such as NVidia, Qualcomm, and Broadcom. They are end-user platforms and behind-the-scenes architecture businesses that enable the metaverses. That's where the most money can potentially be made.

Private businesses and startups aren't included. If you're not a member of the venture capitalist community, you can't invest in these firms. There are many alternative investment options available. Some of them are crowdfunding platforms, while others are focused on investing in specific technologies.

Short-term trading is when you buy and sell securities within a certain period of time. Short-term traders often focus on making quick profits through buying low and selling high. However, there are risks associated with this type of strategy. For instance, if you buy a stock at $100 per share and then sell it at $90 per share, you will lose money. You may also miss out on potential gains if the price of the security increases during the time you own it.

Chapter 7: Web 3.0

Web3, also known as the read-write-trust web, is the third iteration of the internet. It is powered by smart contracts, cryptocurrencies, NFTs, and blockchain technology to create a decentralized web. That means that instead of being centrally controlled, it is distributed through a network of computers to make it more secure as well as resilient. The decentralized web also introduces a change in domain names. It will change domain names from the traditional domain name system (DNS) to a web3 domain name.

Domain Names:-

Web3 domain names, DNS addresses that are blockchain-based, enable users to create as well as manage their personalized domains. They are addresses which represent a user's wallet. The decentralized crypto domain names are NFTs which users may trade on NFT marketplaces. Web3 domain name extensions consist of .crypto, .eth, .blockchain, .dao, .nft, etc. Registering a web3 domain name will require using a domain registrar that supports the service, like Ethereum Name Service (ENS) and Unstoppable Domains.

How to Register:-

Users will need to use an Ethereum wallet that supports ENS when they register a web3 domain name. When the domain is registered, users are able to set up a DNS record for it. This will allow people to find the website or application by using normal domain name lookup tools.

Users should choose wallets supporting ENS that meet their needs. After users have chosen an Ethereum wallet, they will need to register their web3 domain name through a smart contract on the Ethereum blockchain. This is done by using a service like MyEtherWallet. When the domain is registered, users may set up a DNS record for it through services like ENS or Unstoppable Domains. People will be able then to find the websites and applications using regular domain name lookup tools.

The three types of smart contracts utilized by ENS include the registry, the registrars, and the resolvers.

The first type of contract is the registry. It is the top-level contract of the ENS. The registry is responsible for storing all the domain names as well as their associated resolver smart contracts. It also clearly explains the rules that are involved in setting up and maintaining a .eth domain name. This includes aspects such as who has the ability to create one, how long it lasts, how you can renew it, etc.

Another type of contract is a registrar. This is a contract that will allow users to claim as well as manage .eth domains. It maintains domain names and allows users to subdomain names based on criteria. The permanent registrar, which is the registered owner, and the registrar controller, controls the day-to-day activities, the concept allows the name holders the ability to outsource their names. Currently the two types of registrars. They are an open registrar, where you can register your unique domain name, and an auction registrar, where you can bid on domain names.

A resolver is a contract that provides the mapping between an Ethereum address and a .eth domain name. Whenever a user types in an address or username in their browser or wallet, the resolver will produce the Ethereum address associated with it. The domain owner is the person who arranges the resolver contract. It may be updated to change the mapping. In other words, the resolver stores the name-to-record mapping.

What Is ENS and How Does It Work?

The new domain naming system, known as ENS, was built on the Ethereum network. This new system enables users to develop distinctive usernames or addresses. Ethereum's smart contracts are utilized by ENS in an effort to manage domain name registration and resolution as well as offer supplementary services to the traditional DNS. With the new web 3.0 infrastructure, ENS domains have surpassed traditional domain names. ENS domains are capable of creating decentralized websites and applications. They also use the blockchain to store data or files.

ENS provides users with the ability to develop a single username to use for all their decentralized apps, wallet addresses, and websites in a distributed ecosystem.

With the new web 3.0 infrastructure, ENS domains have surpassed traditional domain names. ENS domains are capable of creating decentralized websites and applications. They also use the blockchain to store data or files.

ENS provides users with the ability to develop a single username to use for all their decentralized apps, wallet addresses, and websites in a distributed ecosystem.

Cloud Storage:-

Amazon and Google are the pioneers in cloud computing. On web3.0, many other companies are also offering similar services. Filecoin, sia coin, arweave, and others are just a few examples. People are motivated to store files on the network because they get paid in the native currency of the system.

Data is stored on the blockchain, or it is monitored using smart contracts. For example, sia coin monitors payments to ensure that data is not lost. There are multiple copies of data available, and if someone loses data, they lose their collateral.

The technology that is underlying Bitcoin, known as the Blockchain, has undeniably changed the finance world forever with the creation of a universal and irrefutable decentralized ledger of transactions. Blockchain servers that are stored on multiple computers are replacing centralized servers that hold information, making Web 3.0 blockchain-based. This means that the processing and storage potential of Web 3.0 will greatly surpass anything we have seen before. There will be no single point of authority for the data that is stored in Web 3.0, leading to the decentralization of information.

By doing this, it becomes more secure and more difficult to hack. This democratization of the internet allows it to become less reliant on Big Tech companies and more open-sourced.

The same is true for Ethereum, smart contracts, which are shaping the newest version of the internet, called Web 3.0. Unprecedented possibilities across various fields involving fairness, accessibility, and transparency for all parties can be greatly improved by the decentralization that Ethereum, along with smart contracts technology offer. With the growth of the Decentralized Finance (DeFi) and Non-Fungible Token (NFT) industries, we are witnessing the results for ourselves.

The path towards decentralization won't be an easy one, however. One of the drawbacks that can be observed is the scalability issues that currently plague the Ethereum ecosystem, making simple transactions wind up costing close to 10 dollars, and more complex smart contracts could cost around $100 to execute when the network suffers from congestion.

Chapter 8: Metaverse Medical Technology

Telepresence:-

This is known in healthcare as telemedicine. Telemedicine is the provision of medicine as a remote service. It experienced a surge in popularity during the Covid-19 pandemic.

Before 2020, only 43% of healthcare facilities were able to provide remote treatment to their patients. Today, around 95% of healthcare facilities can provide treatment through telemedicine.

For routine consultations that do not require a physical examination (or that can be done visually), doctors and nurses have discovered that they can quickly and efficiently diagnose many minor conditions that make up the majority of their caseload through a telephone or video call. This will certainly continue in the Metaverse.

Virtual reality, which is a key technology enabling next-level immersion that partly qualifies a platform or application as part of the Metaverse, opens a new range of possibilities. The headset-based VR experience conveys a greater sense of "being there" than any other virtual environment like websites, messaging apps, or social media.

Telemedicine consultations, specifically through VR, mean patients will no longer be limited to being treated by certain clinicians because of their physical location.

Patients in Africa who need specialists to be in India can effectively be in the same place by putting on headsets. Tests and scans are carried out at a local facility near the patient, and the data is transferred to the specialist.

It's especially useful in places like China, where there is a shortage of medical professionals, and patients in remote regions who ordinarily have to travel long distances to be seen by healthcare professionals.

Health Technology:-

Many innovative and original leaps have been made in health technology through the centuries. However, few have had as much notoriety or impact as digital technology. Significant enhancements, networking, and computers have expanded options when it comes to medical treatments. These enhancements have also transformed clinicians performing their jobs.

Although unconventional thinkers began the discussion of the possibility of using computers in the medical field as early as the 1960s, originally, computers were too expensive and too unreliable for medical practices to be able to rely on.

Policies and data standards were created as a way to encourage healthcare organizations to adopt emerging technology as technology has made improvements and the cost has decreased. This was done not only to encourage the use of new medical equipment, such as diagnostic imaging machines but for day-to-day record keeping as well.

With the development of electronic health records (EHRs) digitized medical records replaced paper versions. EHRs make it easier to access health data such as test results or diagnoses adequately and safely.

It is now standard practice to utilize EHR systems or other technologies while interacting with patients and developing treatment plans. It is now just as common to see laptops and tablets during a visit to a healthcare facility as it is to see a stethoscope. There is also increasing evidence that the use of EHRs is having a positive effect on obtaining as well as exchanging health information.

One major challenge EHRs have created is the collection of huge amounts of unintegrated and unstandardized data. The majority of healthcare organizations have an abundance of data they can utilize in an effort to enhance their procedures as well as their business practices. However, they may not have the resources or expertise to discover insights into that information.

Newer technologies, such as blockchain, cloud, and AI tools which are based on machine learning, could assist healthcare organizations in revealing patterns within huge quantities of data. They can also make that data easier to manage and more secure.

Technology solutions are enabling leaders to enhance performance, increase collaboration throughout systems, and manage costs. As the demands on organizations rise, healthcare technology can automate tasks, streamline processes, and enhance overall workflow to a degree that's impossible for humans to accomplish alone.

As practitioners at hospitals and medical facilities have welcomed value-based health reimbursement models, solutions like these are allowing healthcare professionals to enhance patient care, create better experiences and minimize burnout.

Digital Twins:-

A digital twin is a simulation, or virtual model, of any object, system, or process created with the use of real-world data, with the intended purpose of discovering more about its real-world counterpart. In the Metaverse, it is possible for the patient to have a digital twin.

CEO of Latus Health, Jack Latus, who is an online healthcare provider that specializes in occupational health, believes that eventually, digital twins will become the "test dummies" for patients. These digital twins could be used to predict things such as how we are able to recover from surgery or the possible reactions we might have to specific medications.

Our growing ability to map and comprehend an individual's genetics will make this advancement possible. Medical professionals will have the ability to fast-forward to what happens to the patient if they increase the age of the twin by ten years, using the interventions they are currently using. This would allow them to see how it could affect the twin.

Blockchain Technology:-

Blockchain technology is known as the underlying technology of cryptocurrencies such as Bitcoin. In reality, blockchains are just dispersed and encrypted databases. These databases enable data to be stored and transferred safely in a way that can only be changed by the data owner. A majority of people consider blockchains to be an intricate part of the concept of the Metaverse because they make it possible for decentralized communities that are governed democratically through smart contracts, along with a digital record of "ownership" of environments or objects that are in the digital domain. When it comes to healthcare, the most obvious use of blockchain technology is in the management and security of patients' highly sensitive health data. Data is frequently shared between several organizations in a way that is both unclear and inefficient as far as the owners of that information (patients) are concerned. The fact that health records are normally stored on centralized servers means that a patient's information is at risk of being stolen.

On the dark web, a single health record is said to have a resale value of between $70 and $100. That would also mean that getting access to it, even for those who would have a legitimate reason to access it, such as a medical specialist who is treating the patient, is usually a long and tedious process.

Convergence:-

The convergence of core technologies like these in the Metaverse means healthcare professionals will be capable of delivering more joint treatment programs and packages, unobstructed by the isolated nature of the majority of the current healthcare system.

Rapid sharing of information among clinicians would mean that the underlying causes of illnesses would be discovered faster. The monitoring of a patient's activity in the Metaverse would mean that factors like patient compliance could be tracked more easily, which might further help to find a diagnosis and treat the illness. For example, if a patient is being treated by a physiotherapist for an injured knee and no physical damage can be seen then there is a need to search for another reason why it isn't getting better.

It is possible that it could turn out that because of depression that the patient is not doing their physical therapy exercises. This would mean that the physical injury is not going to heal. Providing treatment in a joint manner within a virtual environment along with a new approach to sharing information would make the treatment of this injury quicker and more effective.

Virtual Hospital:-

Another part of the future of healthcare centers around the concept of the "virtual hospital". A virtual hospital is a project that is currently being developed by Latus Healthcare. There is a possibility that it could become available as a service in the coming year. Essentially it comprises a virtual reality hospital environment, accessed through a headset, where treatments will at first be focused on counseling and physiotherapy services.

Physiotherapy will make use of computer vision—for example, using cameras to investigate the range of motion in damaged joints, as well as the progress that patients are making towards recovery. Latus says, "With VR and AR, we're able to give them much better feedback on their process... for example, for someone with a shoulder joint issue, if that shoulder range of motion improves by three percent, as an individual, you probably wouldn't feel that.

"But if you can get it reported back to you, you will actually see it working, and get a plan; if you improve at this rate, you can get back to normal in a certain number of weeks. From a motivation or compliance point of view, that's going to have a massive effect.

You have genuine data to back up the work you've been putting in. it's clear that many aspects of healthcare delivery will be affected by the opportunities offered by the Metaverse. There may be some hurdles to be overcome first, particularly around people's attitudes to receiving treatment online or remotely – which may still be seen as a second-best or backup option by many.

There are also questions around equality of access—VR headsets are not cheap, and if they are required to take part, it could be seen as further contributing to inequality in access to healthcare. There is a possibility it will become available as a service sometime next year. An essential component of a virtual hospital is the provision of physiotherapy via computer vision, with the aim of improving patient outcomes through increased awareness of movements and activities. Virtual hospitals should also focus on counseling and education, as well as social interaction.

It's clear that many aspects of health care delivery will be affected by virtual reality. Some hurdles need to be overcome first, including people's attitudes about accepting treatment online or remotely. Also, there is the question of equity of access. Virtual Reality is expensive equipment and if you require it to receive treatment, that could contribute to inequality in access to health care.

There are many ways virtual reality can help us in our daily lives. We can see what we need to buy, try out different hairstyles, or even just relax. But there are also other ways to use VR technology to improve our healthcare system. For example, doctors can use VR to train medical students before they start practicing. Patients can get a virtual tour of their bodies while undergoing surgery. And hospitals can offer virtual tours of their facilities to potential customers.

Chapter 9: 2040 TECHNOLOGICAL PREDICTION:

Brain-Computer Interfaces (BCIs):-

Brain-computer interfaces (BCIs) offer a distinct technological solution to bypass the impaired motor system. In neurorehabilitation, the BCI may be used to interpret neural signals tied to movement intentions into a constructive feedback for the patient, when they can't create functional movement on their own.

Clinical interest in BCI is rapidly increasing because it would promote rehabilitation to commence sooner following brain damage. It also offers options for patients that are unable to participate in traditional physical therapy.

Considerable challenges with existing BCI performance have prevented its widespread adoption. Recent progress in knowledge and technology provide opportunities to expedite change, as long as clinicians and researchers who utilize BCI agree on standardization of guidelines in regards to protocols and combined efforts to reveal mechanisms.

Given the potential of brain-computer interfaces (BCIs), which can take direct readings of our thoughts, there are clearly important implications concerning privacy. Several countries are already attempting to define neuro-rights to protect mental privacy and to pass laws protecting them.

Last November, a company called Synchron was given regulatory approval by the FDA to conduct tests on human volunteers using its brain implant, Stentrode. Stentrode is a neural implant that is inserted through the jugular vein into the blood vessels that rests on top of the brain.

After it's in position, small electrodes are deployed within the vessel, near the brain's surface. The electrodes can send signals through an infrared transmitter, which is surgically placed into the chest.

Machine-learning algorithms are utilized to parse those signals, enabling paralyzed subjects to perform simple tasks such as moving a cursor on-screen. BCIs can potentially be used to restore, replace, enhance, supplement, or improve the natural output of the central nervous system (CNS), therefore, providing opportunities for a chance of motor rehabilitation from a range of conditions such as spinal cord injury, traumatic brain injury, and even stroke.

To improve the speed and effectiveness of learning BCI control, which should be the top priority for the field, might be improved with multi-stage approaches. This would harness more sensitive neuroimaging technologies within the early learning stages, before making the transition to more practical implementations.

After a stroke, nearly 80% of survivors end up with varying degrees of impairment to the upper limbs. This is a major factor in preventing their participation in normal daily activities, leaving them dependent on caregivers.

Rehabilitation approaches that actively encourage intensive and extended functional use of the paralytic limb results in the greatest rewards in movement capability. The best approaches like constraint-induced movement therapy (CIMT), require the patient to be able to perform an adequate amount of functional movement to have the opportunity to participate.

This is what inhibits severely impaired patients from participating in such rehabilitation. Patients who are in the early weeks following a brain injury and have not yet regained the function would also be unable to participate.

A vital next step toward justifying the clinical use of BCI is the clarification of the neural mechanisms that assist in motor function enhancements.
There is considerable evidence that suggests that early intervention is vital to harnessing the brain's natural processes of recovery.

Therapies that have the ability to support the patient and create the correct functional patterns of brain activity, as well as motor behavior, are desperately needed, throughout the period when patients are unable to bring about actual movement without assistance. Brain-computer interfaces (BCIs) are being seen as a promising approach in the effort to overcome paralysis.

Service Robots Could Be Used Worldwide:-

Due to rising labor costs, a drastic reduction in labor-intense job fields, and the popularity of no-contact services the pandemic initiated, an increasing number of South Korean businesses have begun using front-line service robots. These service robots have even begun replacing humans in performing routine tasks.

The service robot market in South Korea is expected to increase to an accumulative 230,000 robots by 2025, worth 2.8 trillion won, or $2.25 billion, in value, according to market data collected by the International Federation of Robotics. As of 2020, its size had grown almost 35 percent on-year to 857 billion won, surpassing that of industrial robots. The global market for service robots is expected to increase to $74 billion by 2026.

In an effort to meet the increasing demand for automated services, tech, and manufacturing leaders are switching into the service robots sector. The service robot market is still in the early stages when you compare it to the industrial robots markets.

An automated computer program that was designed to perform customer-oriented tasks is programmed into every service robot. Service robots have the ability to perform tasks in places such as restaurants, medical care facilities, and homes, unlike industrial robots, which are normally seen in factories, Naver, a platform provider, opened its new headquarters to develop the very first robot-friendly building in the world. It will be a place where robots can roam the floors freely to deliver parcels and serve people. Artificially intelligent robots will also have the ability to automatically take notes during meetings.

LG Electronics has made the choice to turn its focus to lifestyle-integrated service robots. The company's latest focus has been branching out into the business-to-business market, finishing a lineup of six kinds of its CLOi robot with various purposes such as delivery and cleaning. The latest version has the ability to self-drive as well as sterilize surroundings with the use of ultraviolet lamps.

Quantum Computers:-

Quantum is a general term that refers to the growing field of technologies that utilize quantum mechanics to create radically new abilities within already established fields such as sensing, pharmaceutics, communications, computing, chemistry, and materials research. The word quantum refers to the most minuscule component or entity in a natural system that we explain with the use of quantum mechanics. Quantum aims to push past the boundaries of traditional physics by harnessing the quantum mechanical properties of matter. This could provide entirely new methods of processing information. These methods have the capabilities to be faster as well as more resource-efficient, which would provide us with the opportunity to accomplish things never before done, such as calculating the formation of proteins or anticipating the complicated behavior of financial systems.

Quantum computing promises a more efficient processing power. The ability to process information quicker opens up the opportunity to take fields like fundamental research, optimization, pharmaceuticals, and information technology farther than we ever thought was possible.

There are some expected security risks, however. A large-scale quantum computer has the capability of cracking NSA encryption. A large ongoing challenge is to create security measures that are safe from both classical as well as quantum computers. The advantage of a quantum computer is that it is capable of processing Big Data, which may have consequences when it comes to personal privacy.

To move quantum computing past its niche existence and into the mainstream, we must learn how to isolate quantum systems from their environment more efficiently while learning how to control them to a higher degree of accuracy. There needs to be a reduction in the number of errors observed in quantum computations. Then the system would need to be scaled up to the hundreds of millions of qubits.

Life-like Virtual Assistants Could Be Mainstream:-

Virtual assistants have become a major part of our lives. We talk to them all day long, whether we realize it or not. They help us get directions, check the weather, play music, answer questions, and even cook dinner. Virtual assistants are becoming more and more integrated into our daily lives, and they will continue to grow in popularity as time goes on. Smart devices are becoming more and more important to everyday life, and virtual assistants are at the forefront of this growth.

Machine learning algorithms are used to predict future events based on past observations. These predictions are often used to automate tasks, making them easier to perform. For example, if you ask your phone to remind you when you need to pick up milk, it might suggest a list of nearby grocery stores that sell dairy products. If you ask your car to find the quickest route to work, it might recommend a different route depending on traffic conditions. In both cases, the system learns what you like and doesn't like, then uses that information to make a recommendation.

The market is now seeing a shift in the direction of voice-first interactions. In 2020, Google launched Duplex, which allows users to call businesses and book appointments using only their voices. Apple also introduced Siri Shortcuts, which allow users to create custom commands for their digital assistants. Furthermore, the rise of smart speakers means that people are increasingly interacting with their homes through voice rather than a screen.

The global Voice Virtual Assistant (VA) market size was valued at USD 9.3 billion in 2019 and is expected to reach USD 18.4 billion by 2023, growing at a CAGR of 16.5%. The market is driven by factors such as increasing demand for digital assistance, rising adoption of mobile devices, and the increasing number of internet users globally.

However, high costs associated with the development of voice applications and lack of standardization among different VAs are some of the major challenges faced by the market.

Futuresource Consulting forecasts that the global market for virtual assistants will grow to $26.5bn by 2025, up from $16.3bn in 2019. This represents a compound annual growth rate of 16.7%. By 2025, the market will be split between two major segments – consumer electronics and enterprise applications. In 2020, the consumer electronics segment held more than half of the total market ($12.8bn), followed by enterprise applications ($4.9bn). However, the consumer electronics segment will decline slightly over the next five years, while the enterprise application segment will continue to gain momentum. There will be about 7.5 billion digital voice assistants being in use in the world by 2020.

In addition, there will be about 110 million virtual assistants being used in the US alone. By 2024, there will be about 8.4 billion virtual assistants being used in devices all around the world. These numbers show how quickly the market is growing.

Einstein Telescope:-

The Einstein Telescope was designed to monitor the vibrations that are caused by gravitational waves that occur from colliding black holes.
It has been said that the Einstein Telescope is the most sensitive instrument to be built in the history of astronomy.

This spectacular piece of equipment is expected to be built in tunnels and underground caverns which are located a few hundred meters below Earth's surface.
The Einstein telescope isn't meant to collect light photons or to provide the world with sensational photographs of nebulae and galaxies.

The facility, which will cost approximately €2bill, will instead register gravitational waves, or disturbances in the curvature spacetime that occur throughout the Universe at the speed of light. This occurs as a result of the violent collisions and fusions of ultra-compact neutron stars along with insatiable black holes.

The Einstein Telescope will create a massive equilateral triangle that measures 10km on each of its sides. Intense rays of laser light will travel up and down the arms. Then bounce off mirrors in an effort to gauge the length of the arms and determine if they change by even a fraction of the width of an atomic nucleus. The occurrence of this particular kind of change could mean that a gravitational wave has passed through, causing a brief disruption in the space that surrounds the detector.

The goal is to detect the collision of black holes throughout the entire observable universe. The Einstein Telescope will enable scientists to explore the Universe via gravitational waves along with its cosmic history towards the cosmological dark ages, and shed light on questions about fundamental physics as well as cosmology.

This sophisticated telescope will probe physics near the horizons of black holes. It will also help in the comprehension of the nature of dark matter, such as ancient BHs, axion clouds, dark matter accumulating on compact objects, as well as the nature of dark energy and possible alterations of general relativity on a cosmic scale. By utilizing the telescope's sensitivity and frequency spectrum, the whole population of stellar as well as smaller mass black holes will be accessible across the entire history of the Universe. This will allow us to understand their origin, stellar versus primitive, evolution, as well as population analysis.

The Einstein Telescope will observe the neutron-star inspiral phase along with the commencement of tidal effects with a high signal-to-noise ratio offering a remarkable insight into the inner structure of neutron stars while investigating underlying components of matter in a totally undiscovered system. The magnificent sensitivity that extends to kilohertz frequencies will also enable us to discover details of the merger as well as the post-merger phase. The telescope will operate in collaboration with a new unprecedented creation of electromagnetic observatories covering the spectrum from radio to gamma rays.

The start of construction is expected in 2026, with the goal to begin observations in 2035. Site selection is expected to occur in 2024. Studies of the site characteristics are in progress. The two sites that are being considered are one located in Sardinia and the another one is located in the Euregio Meuse-Rhine.

Establish the First Permanent Lunar Base:-

The Moon landing program was canceled in 1972, but the U.S. government continued to support manned lunar exploration through the National Aeronautics and Space Administration (NASA). In 2009, President Barack Obama announced his plan to send humans back to the Moon by 2020. The Trump administration canceled the 2024 deadline in favor of an undefined "flexible timeline." Since then, NASA has focused on developing technologies needed to get humans to Mars.

The Moon is an important stepping stone toward Mars. We need to get there before we can go anywhere else. The Moon provides us with a unique opportunity to test technologies needed for human exploration of Mars. The Moon also offers us the chance to demonstrate our ability to live and work in space for extended periods of time. These capabilities will be essential for future human exploration of Mars.
Artemis VII will deliver a pressurized lunar rover and a surface habitat to the lunar surface in 2030 and 2031, respectively. These would only be used periodically for however long lunar astronauts' missions last.

Clearly, if the US and its international and commercial partners want to develop a permanent lunar outpost, they need to find a way to get people and cargo to and from the lunar soil that is cheaper and more often than the Orion/SLC system. One idea would be to equip the SpaceX Starship HLS to take astronauts from Earth to the lunar surface. Once the Starship's fuel tanks have been topped up in Earth orbit, a crewed Dragon could launch with the astronauts, dock with the Starship, and transfer the crew. Then the A starship could take the crew to the lunar surface. Analysis suggests that the numbers are feasible.

The first step toward establishing a permanent lunar outpost is to establish a sustainable lunar lander capable of carrying people and cargo to the lunar surface and back again. A reusable spacecraft is necessary because there will be no other vehicles available to carry people and supplies to the Moon.

There are several ways to accomplish this goal. One option is to build a large rocket called the Super Heavy Rocket (SHR). The SHR would be about the size of an aircraft carrier and have a payload capacity of over 100 metric tons. It would be powered by multiple Raptor engines and would be capable of lifting heavy loads into low earth orbit.
Lunar Settlement: One idea would be to outfit a Starship HLS to take astronauts from

Earth to the lunar surface. Once there, they could stay for 3–6 months while doing science and developing technologies for future missions. A second option is to send a SpaceX Crew Dragon to the Moon with an astronaut inside. While docked, the spacecraft could be refueled and then launched again. On its return trip home, the Crew Dragon could land at Kennedy Space Center like any other rocket. Analysis suggests that both ideas are feasible. The advantages of either alternative are that they are cheaper than the planned Space Launch System/Orion system and that they can be executed more often, perhaps twice per year. Having astronauts stay at the lunar surface for three months would be more practical to conduct scientific experiments than a year-long.

Deep-Sea Mining Operations:-

As of right now, Deep-sea mining in international waters is illegal. Scientists, environmental organizations, and many governments would like for it to stay that way. They believe that deep-sea mining could do irreversible damage to one of the planet's most remote ecosystems. It is one of the few places on Earth that has vastly escaped human disruption.

Their pleas have grown more urgent, as international regulators are expected to start issuing deep-sea mining permits as early as the summer of 2023. Activists are actively attempting to enlist supporters from tech companies to United Nations delegates in an effort to prohibit the mining companies from exploiting the seabed.

The argument in favor of deep-sea mining is that as the world moves away from fossil fuels, the growing demand for technologies such as batteries for electric vehicles and solar panels will need massive amounts of nickel, cobalt, and manganese, as well as other clean-energy metals.

Land-based metal reserves are in short supply. They're often located close to communities that are damaged by mining activities. There are billions of dollars worth of these metals sitting at the bottom of the ocean, nowhere near civilization, and no one has taken advantage of them.

It has been argued that, by powering clean-energy technologies and accelerating a shift away from fossil fuels, deep-sea mining will actually protect the oceans from incessant climate change. Growing CO_2 emissions have already caused catastrophic ocean modification, and deoxygenation, along with the reduction of marine species populations across the globe.

The deep sea is among the planet's most obscure places. It is home to tens or even hundreds of thousands of plant and animal species that are still a mystery to humans.

Scientists argue it would be reckless to disturb this environment. Research from the Max Planck Institute for Marine Microbiology indicates that more than half of marine species in the Clarion-Clipperton Zone, a mineral-rich fracture zone that extends 4,500 miles across the bottom of the Pacific Ocean, are reliant on the deep-sea mineral deposits in which mining companies have set their sights on. By removing these deposits, known as polymetallic nodules, we could trigger a torrent of negative effects on the ecosystem.

Recovery would be almost impossible, due to the fact that these nodules take millions of years to develop. Deep-sea mining would also kick up debris from the ocean floor. Scientists worry that clouds of sediment will clog marine species' filtration systems, making it more difficult for them to see through the water. Sonic disturbances caused by mining might also echo far and wide and negatively impact whales as well as other species that depend on sound waves to hunt for prey.

Jeffrey Drazen, a professor of oceanography at the University of Hawaii, Manoa, also warned that the seabed might potentially accelerate climate change by disrupting carbon sequestration dynamics in the deep ocean.

Experts agree that there isn't enough information about the dangers of seabed mining to do so safely. A growing number believe the risks greatly outweigh any potential benefits that might come from deep-sea mining. They argue that the world's clean-energy needs can be accomplished through land-based mining, or through technological breakthroughs. They believe that a drastic improvement in recycling infrastructure may significantly decrease the need for the majority of mining, to begin with.

The deep-sea mining debate began to escalate due to a surprise move from Nauru, which is a small island in the southwestern Pacific Ocean. Last summer, Nauru sent a letter to the International Seabed Authority, or ISA expressing its intent to start mining the seafloor in international waters. This triggered an unknown "two-year rule," that forced the ISA to start issuing deep-sea mining permits by the summer of 2023.

The ISA will try to finalize regulations for seafloor mining before that deadline, but this is not required by law. ISA regulators are expected to open the seabed to mining companies next summer, even without a mining code.

Conclusion

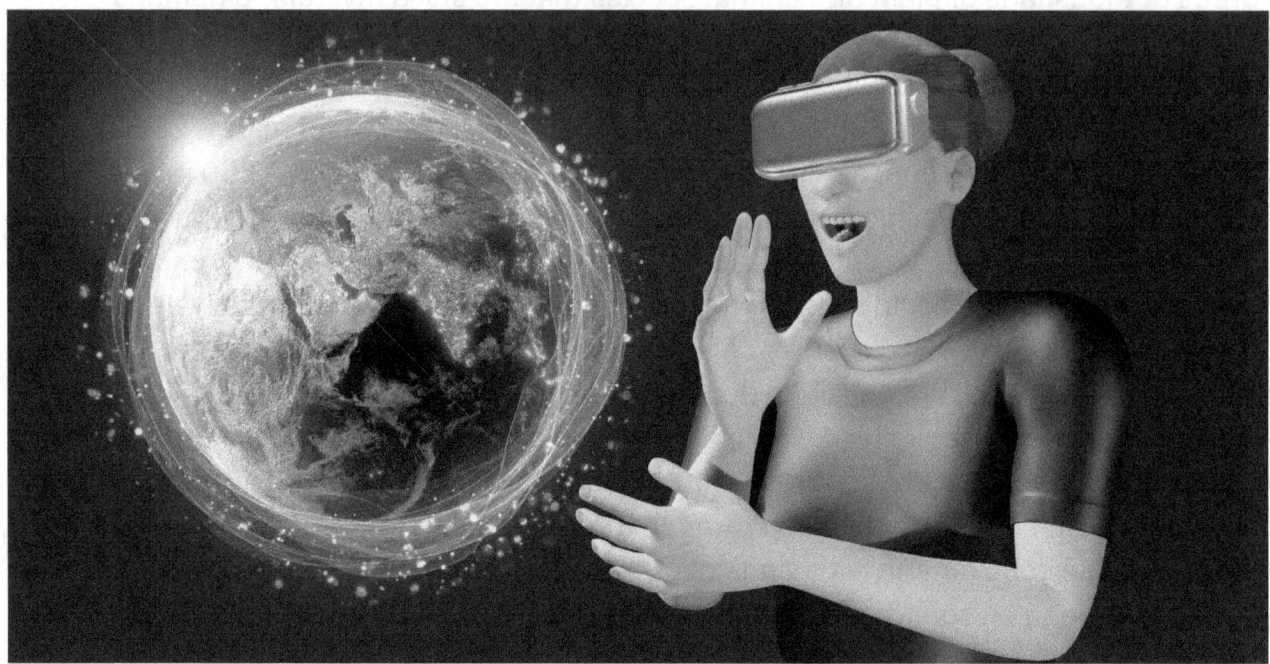

"The Metaverse is a digital environment that will eventually take place in the real world. It is designed to create a safe, secure, connected, and transparent ecosystem for users to conduct any type of transaction. In other words, it is a third dimension that connects our physical reality with the virtual realm."

The Metaverses is a digital environment that replaces or enhances real-world functions. People may go to school, work, study, play, or relax from time to time in the Metaverse. In addition, they may also buy goods online, watch movies, listen to music, read books, or otherwise enjoy themselves.

The Metaverse is meant to be a safe, secure, and connected ecosystem. Users can transact in the Metaverse using various forms of currency, including virtual money, cryptocurrency, fiat money, and credit cards. As a result, the Metaverse is not controlled by any single entity.

There is no central authority to enforce rules and regulations. Instead, there are many different companies that have their own platforms. These platforms are operated independently. Each company has its own rules and policies. For instance, one company may allow certain types of items while another does not. Some companies may charge fees while others do not.

The Metaverse is designed to be open to anyone. However, it is important to note that there are risks associated with entering the Metaverse. For instance, some websites may contain malicious code that could harm your PC.

Also, some websites may ask for personal information such as passwords or credit card numbers. If you enter these sites, you risk having your identity stolen. Therefore, it is best to exercise caution when visiting the Metaverse.

Participants may represent themselves as anyone they choose with their avatars while virtually active in the Metaverse. To paraphrase a sci-fi movie about the Oasis, which describes the Metaverse: "Individuals come to the Metaverse for all the virtual experiences they desire."

Artificial Intelligence (AI) is going to be a big deal in the Metaverse. For example, if you think about the Metaverse as a game, then all of us playing could be considered players.

If we consider ourselves to be the characters within the game, then the AI could be considered the actual game itself.

The AI would be watching everything we do and making adjustments accordingly. Some of the changes could be subtle, like adjusting the difficulty of a level. Others could be drastic, like changing the rules of the game entirely.

But, overall, the Metaverse would become a place where you can interact with other players and the AI at the same time. You could chat with them, trade items, and even fight against each other. All of this would happen seamlessly.

Virtual Reality has become an important tool in education. Virtual worlds allow students to interact with objects and environments in ways that were not possible before. Students can create and modify their own 3D spaces and learn about physics, engineering, architecture, biology, chemistry, art, history, geography, psychology, philosophy, math, and many more topics.

Students can even design and construct their own game levels and share them with others. VR is becoming increasingly affordable, allowing us to create our own experiences at home. It is also possible to make use of existing games like Minecraft and Second Life and even download free virtual worlds.

It's important to remember that the Metaverse isn't just a place; it's also a mindset. If If you're going to survive and thrive in the Metaverse, your mindset needs to change. Your attitude toward life, the way you see the world, and your approach to everything need to shift. For example, if you were previously a pessimist, you'll have to become an optimist.

If you were once a complainer, you'll have to embrace gratitude. If you've always struggled with procrastination, you'll have to learn to get things done.

These are just a few examples. If you're serious about joining the Metaverse, you need to prepare yourself mentally, physically, emotionally, and spiritually.

References

1. Dalton, S. (2022, January 20). *5 Tokens to profit from the Metaverse movement.* Medium. George, M. (2022, March 25). *Star Atlas: Is THIS the Metaverse game everyone wants?* Coin Bureau.

2. Kaur, Harpreet. *Buying land in Sandbox - Is Sandbox land a good investment?* Crypto Bulls Club, 13 Nov. 2021, Accessed 16 June 2022.

3. Moskov, Alex. *What is the Sandbox: A guide to the growing crypto Metaverse.* CoinCentral, 5 Jan. 2022, Accessed 16 June 2022. Purdy, Mark. *How the Metaverse could change work.* Harvard Business Review, 5 Apr. 2022

4. *3 Ways to invest in the early stages of the Metaverse • Benzinga.* (2022, February 15). Benzinga.

5. Illuvium. (2021, June 30). 1. Illuvium — fight for Eth. Illuvium. Music 30

6. Narumi, M. (n.d.). UFO coin price prediction: Will Super Galactic boost the coin? Capital-com.cdn.ampproject.org. Retrieved June 16, 2022